The Ultimate Retirement Guide for 55+ in 2024

Successful Money Management Techniques for a Lifetime

LEWIS MADISON

Table of Contents

PART1: Introduction

Overview and Purpose

Understanding the broad principles and goals that steer this extensive guide is crucial for anybody starting the path to a happy and safe retirement.

Understanding the Landscape

The dynamic field of retirement planning is impacted by social, cultural, and personal issues. This guide offers a current summary of the retirement scene for 2023 and offers insights into new trends and difficulties that people 55 and older may face.

The purpose of the Guide

The principal aim of this guide is to equip readers with the information and techniques required to manage their finances successfully during their retirement years. This guide seeks to provide readers with an easy way for making decisions that are in line with their individual financial circumstances by breaking down intricate financial ideas into practical insights.

Target Audience

This manual is intended mostly for people who are 55 years of age or older and are either in retirement or have already retired. Acknowledging the wide range of financial circumstances and goals that comprise this group, the handbook covers a wide range of subjects to guarantee applicability for individuals at different phases of retirement preparation.

Key Themes Explored

Important topics covered in this guide include risk management, estate planning, income generation, portfolio construction, financial health evaluation, and holistic well-being. Every topic is addressed via a pragmatic perspective, offering readers practical guidance and real-life illustrations to help them navigate the intricacies of retirement preparation.

Guiding Principles

A core understanding of smart financial management is instilled through the introduction of a set of guiding concepts throughout the guide. These ideas are weaved throughout every part to guarantee coherence and consistency in the guidance offered. They act as lighthouses, illuminating the way to financial security.

Roadmap for the Reader

The guide follows a logical progression to make it easier to navigate and understand. It is recommended that readers work through the chapters in order to provide a step-by-step understanding of the many facets of retirement planning. The guide's flexible design allows users to concentrate on particular sections according to their current needs and concerns.

This summary essentially lays the groundwork for a thorough investigation of the subtleties and tactics that constitute the cornerstone of effective money management for people 55 years of age and older in 2023. It is an invitation to set out on a path toward aspirational retirement, financial resilience, and well-informed decision-making.

Financial Landscape: Key Trends in Retirement Planning for 2023

Prolonged Retirement Periods

Retirees are expected to live longer in retirement due to rising life expectancy. Because of this tendency, retirement planning techniques need to change in order to guarantee that financial resources will last for a number of decades.

Implications

Retirees need to reassess their investment portfolios, think about phased retirement plans, and look at ways to generate income in line with a longer retirement period.

Evolving Social Security Dynamics
Retirement planning is impacted by modifications to Social Security benefits and procedures. Comprehending these changes is essential for maximizing Social Security benefits and managing possible obstacles.

Implications
It is important for retirees to be informed about Social Security updates, think about the best ways to collect benefits, and adjust their overall financial planning accordingly.

Technology Integration in Retirement Planning
The use of technology, such as digital financial planning tools and robo-advisors, is revolutionizing the way people approach retirement planning by providing more individualized and accessible options.

Implications
In order to make better decisions, retirees can use technology to simplify financial management, have access to real-time investment analytics, and connect with interactive retirement planning tools.

Continued Focus on Health Care Costs
For seniors, rising healthcare costs continue to be a major issue. It is essential to comprehend the dynamics of healthcare costs if one hopes to preserve financial stability in retirement.

Implications

It is recommended that retirees investigate all available options for complete healthcare coverage, such as Medicare and supplemental insurance, and incorporate healthcare expenses into their overall investment and budgetary goals.

Sustainable and ESG Investing

Investing in Environmental, Social, and Governance (ESG) is becoming more and more popular. An increasing number of retirees are matching their financial portfolios to ethical and sustainable criteria.

Implications

Retirement planning now involves a consideration of sustainable investment options, reflecting a broader awareness of social and environmental impacts alongside financial returns.

Shifting Retirement Age Trends

Trends in retirement age are being influenced by shifting society and economic conditions. Some people are opting to work longer hours, which has an effect on savings plans and retirement income.

Implications

Retirees must adapt to evolving retirement age norms, consider phased retirement options, and align their financial plans with individual choices and workforce trends.

Increased Emphasis on Holistic Well-being
Retirement planning now takes into account holistic well-being, which includes lifestyle choices, mental and physical health, in addition to finances.

Implications
Retirees are encouraged to adopt a holistic approach to retirement planning, integrating strategies for maintaining overall well-being alongside financial management.
In navigating the complex landscape of retirement planning in 2023, staying informed about these key trends is important. Understanding and adapting to these shifts will empower retirees to make informed decisions that align with their financial achievements and aspirations for a secure and fulfilling retirement.

PART II: Financial Health Check

Assessing Your Financial Foundation

Importance of Net Worth Evaluation

An extensive evaluation of your financial situation as seen through the prism of net worth is a crucial first step in retirement preparation. Your net worth, which is the difference between your assets and liabilities, is a measure of your financial situation. This assessment gives you a comprehensive picture of your current financial status while highlighting your strengths and providing suggestions for improvement.

Calculating Net Worth

Make a thorough inventory of all your assets, such as savings, investments, and real estate, and deduct all of your liabilities, such as loans, mortgages, and credit card debt, to determine your net worth. By updating this computation on a regular basis, you can monitor changes over time and get a dynamic picture of your financial development.

Budgeting for Retirement

The foundation of sound financial management is budgeting, particularly as retirement draws near. You can manage spending, distribute resources sensibly, and guarantee financial stability throughout your retirement years by creating a realistic and thorough budget.

Creating a Retirement Budget

Start by evaluating your income sources, such as Social Security, pensions, and investment returns. The basis of your budget is your understanding of your anticipated revenue sources.

Expense Categorization

Sort your spending into categories such as necessities and extras. Give priority to necessities like housing, health care, and daily expenses. Determine the areas where modifying discretionary spending will help you reach your retirement objectives.

Emergency Fund Allocation

Set aside some money for an emergency fund in your budget. By acting as a safety net, this financial cushion enables you to handle unforeseen costs without endangering your long-term financial security.

Long-Term Savings

Even after you retire, keep your long-term savings as a priority. It is advisable to allocate finances for significant costs such as medical care, housekeeping, and possible vacations.

Strategies for Improving Net Worth
Debt Reduction
Reducing and managing high-interest debt well is a major factor in increasing net worth. Make debt repayment plans a priority in order to free up funds for investments and savings.

Investment Diversification
Increasing the potential for returns while reducing risk is achieved through portfolio diversification. Review and modify your investments on a regular basis to ensure they meet your financial objectives and risk tolerance.

Continual Financial Education
It's critical to keep up with market developments, investment opportunities, and retirement planning techniques. Maintaining your financial literacy gives you the ability to make wise decisions that increase your net worth.

Monitoring and Adjusting
Plan recurring financial examinations to examine your wealth, evaluate the success of your spending plan, and make any necessary corrections. Changes in life and the economy may necessitate regular adjustments to your financial plan.

Professional Guidance
Think about consulting with financial advisors who focus on retirement planning. Their observations can offer insightful viewpoints that will help you

adjust your budgeting techniques and net worth to your particular situation.

In conclusion, a thorough financial health check that includes a net worth assessment and careful budgeting is necessary to ensure that retirement planning is successful. To establish and preserve a strong financial base for your retirement years, you must engage in ongoing financial education, make strategic adjustments on a regular basis, and monitor your finances closely.

Net Worth and Budgeting

Net Worth:

A financial metric called net worth gives an overview of the financial health of a person or an organization. It stands for the distinction between liabilities and assets. To put it another way, net worth is the amount that's left over after deducting debt from assets. It can assist you in monitoring your progress toward your financial objectives and serves as a critical gauge of your overall financial situation.

Components of Net Worth:
1. **Assets**:
   Savings accounts, cash, and other easily convertible assets are examples of liquid assets.

-Investments: Real estate, mutual funds, stocks, bonds, and other financial holdings.
-Personal Property: The worth of your house, car, jewelry, and other priceless belongings.

2. **Liabilities:**
- Debts: Credit card balances, auto loans, school loans, mortgages, and any other outstanding debts.

Calculating Net Worth:
To determine your net worth, deduct all of your liabilities from all of your assets:

[Net Worth = (Assets - Liabilities)]

When your assets are greater than your liabilities, your net worth is positive, indicating stability in your finances. On the other hand, a negative net worth indicates financial difficulties because debts exceed assets.

Budgeting:
Making a plan that details your income and expenses is known as budgeting. It acts as a financial road map, assisting you in setting and achieving your financial objectives.

Steps in Budgeting:
1. Determine Financial Goals:
Establish both short- and long-term financial goals. Saving for a trip, clearing debt, or setting up an emergency fund are a few examples.

2. Consider all sources of income, including salary, bonuses, rental income, and investments.

3. List Expenses:
-Sort spending into two categories: variable (entertainment, eating out) and fixed (mortgage, utilities).
-Take into account both necessary and optional expenses.

4. Create the Budget:
-Set aside money for necessities before anything else.
-Set aside a portion of your income for debt repayment and savings.
- Allocate the remaining money to the categories of discretionary spending.

5. Monitor and Adjust:
-Continue to monitor expenditures in relation to the budget.
-Modify the spending plan in response to unforeseen costs or changes in income.

Social Security and Pension Analysis

In order to guarantee people's financial security in retirement, social security and pension systems are essential. These programs are intended to act as a safety net, giving retired people and people with disabilities financial assistance. We will explore the complexities of the social security and pension systems in this in-depth analysis, looking at their designs, purposes, difficulties, and possible future advancements.

Social Security Systems

1. Overview:
   -The purpose of the government program Social Security is to give retired and disabled people financial support.
   - It operates on a pay-as-you-go system, where current workers' contributions fund the benefits for current retirees.

2. Components:
   - Old-Age and Survivors Insurance (OASI): Provides benefits to retirees and their survivors.
   - Disability Insurance (DI): Offers financial assistance to individuals with disabilities.
   - Medicare: Healthcare coverage for individuals aged 65 and older.

3. Funding Mechanism:
   - Social Security is primarily funded through payroll taxes, with employees and employers contributing a specific percentage of income.

4. Challenges:
   - Demographic Shifts: Aging populations can strain the system as the number of retirees increases.
   - Funding Gaps: Concerns about the sustainability of funding, especially with changing demographics.

Pension Systems

1. Types of Pension Plans:
   - Defined Benefit Plans: Guarantee a specific benefit amount upon retirement.
   - Defined Contribution Plans: Specify the contribution amount, with the ultimate benefit depending on investment performance.

2. Employer-Sponsored Pensions:
   - As part of their benefits package for employees, many employers provide pension plans.
   - The responsibility for managing investments and ensuring solvency lies with the employer or a pension fund.

3. Individual Retirement Accounts (IRAs) and 401(k)s:

- Self-directed retirement savings accounts that individuals contribute to voluntarily.
- Offer tax advantages and empower individuals to manage their retirement investments.

4. Challenges:
- Funding Volatility: Market fluctuations can impact the performance of pension investments.
- Shift to Defined Contribution Plans: Employers are increasingly favoring these plans, shifting more responsibility to individuals.

Comparative Analysis

1. Risk and Security:
- Social Security offers a secure, government-backed safety net.
- Pension plans carry investment risks, with returns dependent on market performance.

2. Flexibility:
- Social Security provides a stable income based on a predetermined formula.
- Pension plans may offer more flexibility in terms of contributions and investment choices.

3. Influence of Economic Factors:
- Economic conditions impact both systems, affecting funding levels and benefit adequacy.

Future Developments and Recommendations:

1. Policy Adjustments:
   - Regular reviews and adjustments to retirement age, tax rates, and benefit formulas to ensure long-term sustainability.

2. Innovations in Pension Plans:
   - Exploring new pension plan models that balance employer and individual responsibilities.

3. Technological Integration:
   - Utilizing technology to streamline administration, reduce costs, and enhance the efficiency of pension systems.

Conclusion

The examination of the pension and social security systems concludes by highlighting their critical roles in ensuring retirement stability. It is imperative to tackle obstacles and adjust to evolving demographics and economic circumstances to guarantee the sustained efficacy of these mechanisms in protecting the fiscal welfare of retired and disabled persons. It is critical to continue being watchful and proactive in determining the future of the social security and pension systems, even as we celebrate the accomplishments of the previous year.

Healthcare Planning for Retirement

As people get closer to retirement, careful healthcare planning becomes essential to guaranteeing a safe and happy life after work. Having a well-designed healthcare plan protects against escalating medical expenses and also plays a major role in preserving general health. The goal of this guide is to give a thorough and expert overview of retirement healthcare planning, including important factors, methods, and resources.

Assessing Current Health Status

1. Medical Checkup:
  - Schedule a thorough medical checkup before retirement to assess your current health status.
  - Identify and address any existing health concerns.

2. Healthcare History:
- Compile a detailed healthcare history, including medications, vaccinations, and chronic conditions.
- Share this information with your primary care physician to develop a proactive healthcare strategy.

Understanding Medicare

1. Enrollment Timing:

- Familiarize yourself with Medicare enrollment periods, beginning three months before turning 65.

- Timely enrollment helps avoid penalties and ensures comprehensive coverage.

2. Medicare Parts:

- Understand the different parts of Medicare - Part A (Hospital Insurance), Part B (Medical Insurance), Part C (Medicare Advantage), and Part D (Prescription Drug Coverage).

- Determine which sections correspond to your medical requirements.

3. Supplemental Coverage:

- Consider supplementary Medigap policies to cover expenses not addressed by basic Medicare plans.

- Assess Medicare Advantage plans for additional benefits.

Financial Planning for Healthcare

1. Budgeting for Healthcare Costs:

- Estimate annual healthcare expenses and incorporate them into your retirement budget.

- Consider potential out-of-pocket costs, premiums, and prescription drug expenses.

2. Health Savings Accounts (HSAs):

- Contribute to an HSA before retirement to cover qualified medical expenses tax-free.

- Utilize HSA funds strategically for medical costs in retirement.

Long-Term Care Planning

1. Long-Term Care Insurance:
- Evaluate the need for long-term care insurance to cover potential nursing home or home healthcare expenses.
- Compare policies and consider inflation protection.

2. Advance Healthcare Directives:
 - Draft advance directives, such as living wills and healthcare proxies, to outline your preferences for medical care in case of incapacity.
- Share these directives with family members and healthcare providers.

Wellness and Preventive Measures

1. Maintaining a Healthy Lifestyle:
 - Emphasize preventive care, regular exercise, and a balanced diet to promote overall health.
 - Engage in activities that enhance mental and emotional well-being.

2. Preventive Screenings:
- Schedule regular preventive screenings recommended for your age group and health condition.

- Stay proactive in managing health to detect potential issues early.

Conclusion

Preventive measures should be prioritized, healthcare options should be understood, and financial readiness are all important components of comprehensive retirement healthcare planning. People can protect their health, reduce financial risk, and have a happy and healthy retirement by being proactive. To further ensure that the healthcare plan is effective in meeting changing needs, it should be reviewed on a regular basis and adjusted as circumstances change.

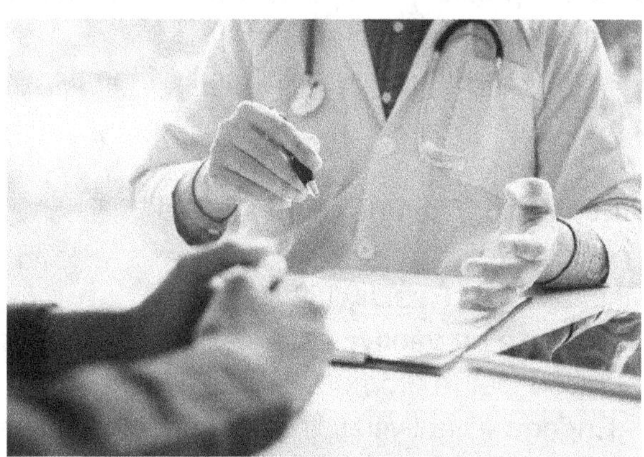

PART III: Building a Retirement Portfolio

Investment Strategies

A key component of financial planning is creating a retirement portfolio, which will guarantee a comfortable and secure future. A carefully managed, well-diversified portfolio can supply the money you need to maintain your retirement lifestyle. This is a comprehensive guide to assist you in creating a retirement portfolio that works:

Step 1: Define Your Retirement Goals

Before you start building your portfolio, it's essential to have a clear understanding of your retirement goals. Consider factors such as the age at which you plan to retire, your desired lifestyle, and any specific financial milestones you want to achieve during retirement.

Step 2: Assess Your Risk Tolerance

Understanding your risk tolerance is crucial for constructing a portfolio that aligns with your financial comfort level. Your age, financial status, and personal preferences are some of the things that affect your risk tolerance. Generally, younger investors can afford to take on more risk, while those closer to retirement might prefer a more conservative approach.

Step 3: Determine Your Time Horizon

The time until your retirement is a critical factor in portfolio construction. A longer time horizon typically allows for a more aggressive investment strategy, including a higher allocation to equities. Conversely, if you're nearing retirement, a more conservative approach with a focus on capital preservation may be appropriate.

Step 4: Asset Allocation

The process of allocating your investment portfolio among various asset classes, including cash, bonds, and stocks, is known as asset allocation. Your time horizon, financial objectives, and risk tolerance will determine the best combination. Commonly, a diversified portfolio includes a combination of stocks for growth, bonds for income and stability, and cash for liquidity.

- Stocks (Equities): Historically, stocks have provided the highest returns over the long term. They also come with higher volatility. Consider a mix of large-cap and small-cap stocks across various sectors.

- Bonds (Fixed-Income): Bonds offer stability and regular interest income. In general, people view them as less hazardous than stocks. Choose a mix of government and corporate bonds with varying maturities.

- Cash (Liquidity): Maintaining some cash or cash equivalents provides liquidity and ensures you have funds available for emergencies or immediate needs.

Step 5: Diversification

To lower risk, diversification entails distributing your investments among a variety of assets. Don't concentrate your portfolio in one or a few assets, as this could expose you to essential volatility. Diversification can be achieved by investing in different sectors, geographic regions, and asset classes.

Step 6: Regular Rebalancing

Make sure your portfolio is in line with your goals and risk tolerance by reviewing and adjusting it on a regular basis. Your asset allocation may stray from your goal due to market fluctuations. To maintain your intended allocation, rebalancing entails selling overperforming assets and purchasing underperforming ones.

Step 7: Tax-Efficient Investing

Consider the tax implications of your investments. Utilize tax-advantaged accounts such as 401(k)s, IRAs, or other retirement accounts to maximize tax efficiency. Be conscious of capital gains taxes when rebalancing your portfolio.

Step 8: Stay Informed and Seek Professional Advice

The world of finance changes all the time, so being educated is essential. Keep abreast of economic trends, market conditions, and changes in financial regulations. If needed, consult with a financial advisor to ensure your retirement portfolio aligns with your goals and remains resilient to market fluctuations.

Step 9: Emergency Fund

Maintain a separate emergency fund outside your retirement portfolio. This fund should cover three to six months' worth of living expenses and act as a financial safety net in case of unexpected expenses or job loss.

Step 10: Monitor and Adjust

Regularly monitor your portfolio's performance and adjust your strategy as needed. Life circumstances, economic conditions, and personal goals can change, requiring adjustments to your retirement plan.

You can create a retirement portfolio that is well-suited to your unique needs, risk tolerance, and financial goals by following these steps. Remember that there is always some risk involved in investing, so you should always base your decisions on careful thought and in-depth research.

If you're unsure, consult financial experts to make sure your retirement plan stays on course.

Real Estate Considerations

Real estate transactions are intricate procedures that need to be carefully thought out in order to guarantee success and reduce risks. Knowing the important factors is crucial whether you are a seasoned investor, first-time home buyer, or real estate agent. The goal of this guide is to give a thorough overview of all the important variables related to real estate transactions.

1. **Market Analysis**:
Begin by conducting a thorough analysis of the current real estate market. Understand local trends, property values, and economic indicators. Consider factors like supply and demand, employment rates, and infrastructure development. A robust market analysis forms the foundation for informed decision-making.

2. **Financial Preparedness**:
Examine your financial position and establish a clear budget. Factor in costs beyond the property's purchase price, such as closing costs, property taxes, and maintenance expenses. If financing is needed, explore mortgage options, interest rates, and loan terms. Being financially prepared ensures a smoother transaction process.

3. **Property Type and Purpose**:

Define your goals for the property. Do you want to buy for yourself, as an investment, or for both?? Different property types, such as residential, commercial, or industrial, serve distinct purposes. Consider the potential for future growth or changes in property use.

4. **Location Considerations**:

Location is a critical factor influencing property value and desirability. Evaluate the neighborhood's safety, amenities, proximity to schools, workplaces, and public services. Research future development plans that might impact the area positively or negatively.

5. **Legal Due Diligence**:

Engage legal professionals to conduct a thorough due diligence process. This includes title searches, zoning regulations, environmental assessments, and any legal restrictions on the property. Ensure compliance with local laws and regulations to avoid legal complications later.

6. **Inspection and Condition**:

Invest in a professional property inspection to identify potential issues. Inspect the property's structural integrity, electrical and plumbing systems, and overall condition. This step is crucial for negotiating repairs or adjustments to the property's price.

7. **Negotiation Skills**:
In real estate transactions, having strong negotiating abilities is crucial. Understand the art of compromise and leverage, whether you are a buyer or a seller. Be prepared to negotiate on price, closing dates, and contingencies.

8. **Long-Term Investment Potential**:
If you're considering real estate as an investment, analyze the property's long-term potential. Research the historical appreciation rates in the area, potential rental income, and the overall economic outlook. A strategic investment can yield substantial returns over time.

9. **Risk Mitigation**:
Determine and reduce any risks that might be connected to the property.This includes assessing market volatility, potential legal disputes, or unexpected property value fluctuations. Make backup plans in case something goes wrong.

10. **Future Resale Value**:
Even if you don't plan to sell immediately, consider the property's future resale value. Factors like location, market trends, and property improvements can significantly impact resale potential.

Conclusion
Transactions involving real estate require a thorough and planned approach. Making well-informed decisions that result in favorable

outcomes requires careful consideration of the market dynamics, financial readiness, legal considerations, and long-term objectives. Reaching your goals in real estate requires careful and strategic navigation, whether you're a buyer, seller, or investor.

Tax-efficient Investments

One of the most important factors in creating a winning investing strategy is tax efficiency. Investors can minimize the impact of taxes on their overall portfolio and maximize returns by making strategic choices about tax-efficient investments. The goal of this guide is to give a thorough overview of tax-efficient investing, covering important ideas, tactics, and particular investment vehicles.

Understanding Tax Efficiency

Tax efficiency refers to the ability of an investment to generate returns while minimizing the tax implications for the investor. The goal is to legally reduce the tax liability associated with investment gains, income, and transactions. Several factors contribute to the tax efficiency of an investment:

1. **Tax-Deferred Growth**:

Investments that allow for tax-deferred growth can postpone taxes until a later date. This is particularly advantageous because it allows the investment to compound without the drag of ongoing tax liabilities.

2. **Tax-Advantaged Accounts**:

Utilizing tax-advantaged accounts, such as Individual Retirement Accounts (IRAs), 401(k)s, or other retirement savings plans, can provide significant tax benefits. Contributions to these accounts are often tax-deductible, and earnings grow tax-deferred until withdrawal.

3. **Capital Gains Efficiency**:

It's critical to minimize capital gains taxes. In general, long-term capital gains have a lower tax rate than short-term gains. The timing and type of capital gains can be optimally managed with the aid of strategic portfolio management.

4. **Tax-Efficient Asset Location**:

Placing investments strategically across taxable and tax-advantaged accounts is known as tax-efficient asset location. This approach involves allocating tax-inefficient assets, like taxable bonds, to tax-advantaged accounts and tax-efficient assets, like stocks, to taxable accounts.

Strategies for Tax-Efficient Investing

1. **Buy and Hold Strategy**:
A long-term buy-and-hold strategy can minimize the frequency of taxable events. Investors who hold onto investments for more than a year may qualify for lower long-term capital gains tax rates.

2. **Tax-Loss Harvesting**:
Selling investments that have lost money is part of this strategy, which is meant to balance gains in other parts of the portfolio. Through calculated loss realization, investors can lower their taxable income.

3. **Dividend Investing**:
Focusing on investments with qualified dividends, which are taxed at lower rates, can enhance tax efficiency. Additionally, considering tax-efficient dividend-paying stocks can contribute to a steady income stream.

4. **Municipal Bonds**:
Municipal bonds are often tax-free at the federal level and, in few cases, at the state level. Including these bonds in a portfolio can provide tax-exempt income.

Tax-Efficient Investment Vehicles

1. Index Funds and ETFs:
Exchange-traded funds (ETFs) and passively managed index funds typically produce lower capital gains than actively managed funds. Investors may have reduced tax obligations as a result of this.

2. Roth IRAs:
Roth IRAs offer tax-free withdrawals in retirement, making them an attractive option for tax-efficient investing. Contributions to Roth IRAs are made with after-tax dollars, but qualified withdrawals, including earnings, are tax-free.

3. 529 Plans:
These plans, designed for education savings, offer tax-free withdrawals for qualified educational expenses. Contributions are not tax-deductible at the federal level, but some states offer state income tax benefits.

4. Health Savings Accounts (HSAs):
HSAs offer three tax benefits: tax-deductible contributions, tax-free earnings growth, and tax-free withdrawals for approved medical costs. Because of this, HSAs are an effective tool for tax efficiency and healthcare planning.

Conclusion

A complex process, tax-efficient investing entails carefully weighing a range of investment vehicles and strategies. Investors can minimize the impact of taxes on their wealth while maximizing their overall returns and achieving their financial objectives by integrating tax efficiency into their investment decisions. It is advisable to speak with a tax expert or financial advisor to create a customized tax-efficient investing plan based on unique objectives and circumstances.

PART IV: Income Generation

Diversifying Income Sources

In a time of economic uncertainty, diversifying one's sources of income has become a crucial tactic for people looking to strengthen their financial position. Individuals who depend solely on one source of income are subject to inherent risks, so it is essential to take a diversified approach. This in-depth manual examines the idea of income diversification and offers thorough explanations of tactical approaches to building a stable and secure financial portfolio.

1. Understanding Income Diversification:

In order to reduce the risks associated with relying too heavily on one source of income, income diversification entails the strategic distribution of resources across multiple streams. The objective is to build a well-balanced portfolio that is resilient to changes in the economy, volatility in the labor market, and unforeseen financial difficulties.

2. Building Multiple Income Streams:

Employment Income:

While traditional employment is a primary income source, individuals can explore opportunities for career advancement, additional responsibilities, or skill development to increase earning potential.

Investment Income:
Allocating funds to a diverse range of investments, including stocks, bonds, real estate, and mutual funds, provides an avenue for passive income through dividends, interest, and capital gains.

Entrepreneurial Ventures:
Initiating a side business or entrepreneurial venture allows individuals to tap into their skills and passions, creating an additional income stream. This could range from freelance work to launching a small business.

Passive Income Streams:
Developing passive income sources, such as royalties, affiliate marketing, or investments in income-generating assets, provides a steady stream of earnings with minimal ongoing effort.

3. **Risk Management and Analysis**:

Risk Assessment:
Conducting a thorough risk assessment is crucial to understand potential downsides associated with each income stream. Assessing market trends, industry stability, and personal risk tolerance helps in making informed decisions.

Emergency Fund:
Maintaining an emergency fund is vital to cover unforeseen expenses and navigate periods of income disruption without jeopardizing financial stability.

4. Skill Development and Continuous Learning:

Professional Growth:
Investing in education and skill development enhances employability and opens doors to higher-paying opportunities. Continuous learning ensures relevance in a rapidly evolving job market.

Adaptability:
Being adaptable and open to acquiring new skills positions individuals to explore emerging industries and capitalize on evolving market demands.

5. Strategic Financial Planning:

Budgeting:
Developing a comprehensive budget enables individuals to allocate resources efficiently, identifying surplus funds that can be directed towards investment or debt reduction.

Financial Advisors:
Seeking guidance from financial advisors can provide personalized strategies tailored to individual financial goals, risk tolerance, and timelines.

Conclusion:

The process of diversifying sources of income is intricate and dynamic, requiring constant observation, a strategic mindset, and flexibility in response to shifting market conditions. People can create a strong financial foundation that can withstand adversity and promote long-term prosperity by adopting a diverse approach to income generation. It is a financial well-being investment that yields benefits such as security, flexibility, and stability.

Part-time Work Opportunities

The employment landscape has broadened beyond the conventional confines of full-time employment as people get closer to retirement. Working part-time after retirement has become a popular and exciting alternative that provides a transition from a full-time job to total retirement. This in-depth article delves into the complexities of part-time employment options for retirees, highlighting the benefits, appropriate sectors, and important factors to take into account for individuals looking for a flexible and meaningful post-career phase.

Advantages of Part-Time Work in Retirement:

1. Supplemental Income:
Part-time work allows retirees to supplement their income, providing financial stability while still enjoying the benefits of retirement savings and pensions. This additional income stream can support travel, hobbies, or other personal pursuits.

2. Mental Stimulation:
Engaging in part-time work provides ongoing mental stimulation and a sense of purpose. It allows retirees to leverage their expertise and skills, maintaining cognitive health and staying connected with the professional world.

3. Flexible Schedules:
Part-time roles typically offer flexible schedules, allowing retirees to balance work commitments with leisure activities, family time, and travel. This flexibility enhances the overall quality of life during retirement.

4. Social Interaction:
Part-time work provides opportunities for social interaction and networking, mitigating the potential isolation that some retirees may experience. Building new connections in a workplace setting contributes to a vibrant and active retirement.

Industries Offering Part-Time Opportunities for Retirees:

1.Consulting and Advisory Roles:
Retirees often possess a wealth of knowledge and experience. Consulting and advisory roles allow them to share their expertise on a part-time basis, providing valuable insights to businesses and organizations.

2. Education and Training:
Part-time opportunities in education, such as tutoring or teaching specialized workshops, enable retirees to contribute to the learning community while maintaining a flexible schedule.

3. Nonprofit and Community Engagement:
Many nonprofits welcome retirees for part-time roles, leveraging their skills for community development, fundraising, or advocacy. This sector aligns with retirees' desire to give back and make a positive impact.

4. Remote and Online Opportunities:
The rise of remote work has opened up various part-time opportunities in areas like freelance writing, virtual assistance, and online consulting. Retirees can work from the comfort of their homes, catering to their preferences and lifestyle.

Key Considerations for Retirees Exploring Part-Time Work:

1. Balancing Work and Leisure:

Retirees should carefully balance part-time work commitments with leisure activities and personal pursuits to ensure a harmonious retirement experience.

2. Financial Planning:
Consider the impact of part-time income on overall financial planning, including taxes, Social Security, and any potential effects on pension benefits.

3. Health Insurance and Benefits:
Assess the availability of health insurance and other benefits with part-time roles. Some employers offer benefits to part-time employees, contributing to overall well-being in retirement.

Conclusion:
Retirement-related part-time employment gives a flexible and nuanced approach to the post-career phase, fostering social interaction, mental stimulation, and financial support. Through cautious exploration of the variety of part-time options available, retirees can carve out a career path that fits their objectives, dreams, and longing for a meaningful and fulfilling retirement.

PART V: Estate Planning

Comprehensive Estate Plans

In order to guarantee the efficient transfer of wealth and management of resources in the event of incapacity or death, comprehensive estate planning is an essential process that entails the meticulous organization and structuring of one's assets, liabilities, and general financial affairs. A well-designed estate plan includes more than just writing a will; it includes a number of legal tools and techniques to safeguard and allocate assets in accordance with a person's wishes while reducing tax consequences.

1. Wills and Trusts:
 - A cornerstone of estate planning, a will outlines how a person's assets should be distributed upon their death. It appoints an executor to carry out these wishes and may include guardianship provisions for minor children.
- Trusts, on the other hand, provide more flexibility and control. They allow for the management of assets during one's lifetime and specify conditions under which beneficiaries can access these assets.

2. Power of Attorney:
- Designating a power of attorney is vital for addressing financial and legal matters in case of incapacity. This document authorizes a trusted individual to make decisions on behalf of the incapacitated person.

3. Healthcare Directives:
 - Advanced healthcare directives, such as a living will and healthcare power of attorney, articulate one's preferences for medical treatment in the event of incapacitation. This ensures that healthcare decisions align with personal values.

4. Tax Planning:
 - Estate taxes can significantly impact the wealth transferred to beneficiaries. Comprehensive estate planning involves strategies to minimize tax liabilities, such as gifting strategies, charitable giving, and leveraging exemptions.

5. Beneficiary Designations:
 - Updating beneficiary designations on financial accounts, life insurance policies, and retirement plans is crucial to ensure that assets pass smoothly to intended recipients outside of probate.

6. Business Succession Planning:
 - For business owners, estate planning includes strategies for the seamless transfer of ownership and management to successors. This may involve creating buy-sell agreements or establishing a family limited partnership.

7. Asset Protection:
 - Implementing measures to shield assets from potential creditors is an essential aspect of

comprehensive estate planning. This may involve the use of certain trusts and legal structures.

8. Regular Review and Updates:
 - Making an estate plan is a continuous process. Regular reviews and updates are necessary to account for changes in personal circumstances, tax laws, or family dynamics.

9. Communication and Education:
 - It is crucial to communicate the details of the estate plan with family members and beneficiaries. Education about the implications of the plan can help prevent misunderstandings and disputes.

10. Professional Guidance:
- Consulting with legal, financial, and tax professionals is highly recommended during the estate planning process. These experts can provide specialized advice and ensure that the plan aligns with current laws and regulations.

In conclusion, to protect one's legacy and provide for loved ones in a structured and tax-efficient way, a comprehensive estate plan entails a holistic approach that takes into account legal, financial, and personal aspects. A successful estate planning strategy requires both professional guidance and regular updates.

Family Involvement and Discussions

Family involvement and open discussions play a pivotal role in effective retirement planning. A well-coordinated approach ensures that all family members are on the same page regarding financial goals, expectations, and lifestyle choices during the retirement years. Here's a detailed overview of the importance of family involvement and discussion in the context of retirement:

1. **Establishing Shared Goals**:
- Begin by involving family members in the goal-setting process for retirement. Discuss the desired lifestyle, travel plans, and any specific financial milestones. This ensures that everyone has a clear understanding of the family's vision for retirement.

2. **Financial Transparency**:
- Open and honest communication about current financial situations and retirement savings is crucial. Share details about savings, investments, and any existing retirement accounts. This transparency helps in setting realistic expectations and identifying potential gaps in financial preparedness.

3. **Budgeting for Retirement**:
- Collaborate on creating a comprehensive budget for retirement. Consider ongoing expenses, healthcare costs, and potential leisure activities. Involving the family in this process fosters a sense of ownership and responsibility for financial decisions.

4. **Healthcare and Long-Term Care Planning**:
- Discussing healthcare and long-term care needs is vital. Address potential medical expenses, insurance coverage, and any plans for assisted living or nursing care. Family members can provide valuable input and support in making these important decisions.

5. **Estate Planning and Inheritance**:
- Involve family members in discussions about estate planning, including the distribution of assets and inheritance wishes. Clear communication can help prevent misunderstandings and disputes among heirs.

6. **Social Security and Pension Considerations**:
- Understand the implications of social security benefits and any pension plans. Discuss the timing of claiming social security benefits and how it aligns with overall retirement income strategies.

7. **Roles and Responsibilities**:
- Clarify roles and responsibilities within the family regarding financial management during retirement.

This includes designating decision-makers, power of attorney, and healthcare proxies. Having these conversations in advance can avoid confusion during challenging times.

8. Adapting to Changing Circumstances:
- Life is dynamic, and circumstances may change. Discuss how the family plans to adapt to unforeseen events, such as health issues, market fluctuations, or changes in living arrangements. Flexibility and preparedness are key components of a robust retirement plan.

9. Educating the Family:
- Foster financial literacy within the family, especially among younger members. This includes understanding investment basics, the importance of saving, and the potential impact of inflation. Education ensures that the knowledge and values associated with responsible financial planning are passed down through generations.

10. Regular Check-Ins:
- Establish a routine for regular family meetings to review and adjust the retirement plan as needed. This ongoing dialogue ensures that everyone remains informed and involved in the evolving aspects of retirement planning.

PART VI: Managing Risks

Retirement planning involves careful consideration of potential risks that could impact financial security during one's post-employment years. Effective risk management is essential to ensure a comfortable and stable retirement. Here are key aspects to consider:

1. **Market Risk**:
-Definition: The risk of financial loss due to market fluctuations.
-Management Strategy: Diversify investments across asset classes, such as stocks, bonds, and real estate, to mitigate the impact of market volatility.

2. **Inflation Risk**:
-Definition: The risk that the purchasing power of money will decrease over time.
-Management Strategy: Invest in assets that historically outpace inflation, like equities, and consider inflation-adjusted retirement income options.

3. **Longevity Risk**:
 Definition: The risk of outliving one's retirement savings.
-Management Strategy: Plan for a longer life expectancy, consider longevity insurance, and regularly reassess financial needs.

4. **Healthcare Costs**:
- Definition: The risk of unexpected medical expenses impacting retirement funds.
- Management Strategy: Invest in health insurance and explore long-term care insurance options to mitigate healthcare-related financial risks.

5. **Sequence of Returns Risk**:
- Definition: The risk of poor investment returns early in retirement.
- Management Strategy: Have a diversified portfolio and consider a bucket strategy, allocating funds for different time horizons to manage withdrawal timing.

6. **Interest Rate Risk**:
- Definition: The risk of changes in interest rates affecting fixed-income investments.
- Management Strategy: Diversify fixed-income investments and consider laddering bonds to spread interest rate risk.

7. **Taxation Risk**:
- Definition: The risk of changes in tax laws affecting retirement income.
- Management Strategy: Stay informed about tax regulations, diversify tax-efficiently, and consider consulting a tax professional.

8. **Cognitive Decline Risk**:
- Definition: The risk of mental decline impacting financial decision-making.

- Management Strategy: Establish a power of attorney, involve trusted family members, and consider financial products with built-in safeguards.

9. **Liquidity Risk**:
- Definition: The risk of not being able to access funds when needed.
- Management Strategy: Maintain a liquid emergency fund and ensure a balanced allocation between liquid and illiquid assets.

10. **Social Security and Pension Risks**:
- Definition: The risk of changes in government policies or pension fund stability.
- Management Strategy: Stay informed about policy changes, diversify income sources, and consider alternative income streams.

Through a thorough management of these risks, people can design a flexible retirement plan that can adjust to changing conditions, protecting their financial security and guaranteeing a comfortable retirement lifestyle. For the risk management plan to continue to be effective over time, regular reviews and modifications are essential.

Longevity Risk and Withdrawal Strategies

1. **Understanding Longevity Risk**:
- Definition: Longevity risk refers to the potential financial challenges individuals may face due to outliving their retirement savings.
- Significance: With increasing life expectancy, effective management of longevity risk is crucial to ensure financial security throughout one's retirement years.

2. **Factors Influencing Longevity Risk**:
- Healthcare Advancements: Improvements in medical care contribute to longer life expectancies.
- Lifestyle Choices: Healthy living can impact overall well-being and potentially extend life.
- Genetic Factors: Individual genetic makeup can influence life expectancy.

3. **Withdrawal Strategies to Mitigate Longevity Risk**:

a. Systematic Withdrawal Plan (SWP):
 - Definition:A predetermined withdrawal amount at regular intervals.
 - Advantages: Provides a steady income stream, minimizes the impact of market fluctuations.

b. Bucket Strategy:
- Definition: Allocating retirement assets into different "buckets" based on time horizon and risk tolerance.
- Advantages: Helps manage market volatility, ensures short-term needs are met while maintaining long-term growth potential.

c. Dynamic Withdrawal Approach:
- Definition: Adjusting withdrawal rates based on portfolio performance and life expectancy.
- Advantages:Allows for flexibility in response to market conditions and personal circumstances.

d. Guaranteed Income Solutions:
- Definition:Annuities or pension-like products providing a guaranteed income for life.
- Advantages: Offers a predictable income stream, effectively addresses longevity risk.

4. **Factors to Consider in Withdrawal Planning**:

a. Inflation Protection:
- Importance: Long retirements may be impacted by the eroding effect of inflation.
- Strategy: Opt for investments or financial products that offer inflation-adjusted returns.

b. Investment Allocation:
- Importance: The mix of assets in a portfolio affects long-term growth and risk.

- Strategy: Diversify investments to balance risk and return, adjusting allocations based on changing circumstances.

c. Healthcare Planning:
- Importance: Rising healthcare costs can significantly impact retirement funds.
- Strategy: Allocate funds for potential medical expenses and consider insurance options to mitigate healthcare-related risks.

5. **Regular Review and Adjustment**:
- Importance: Financial markets, personal circumstances, and economic conditions change over time.
 - Strategy: Periodically reassess retirement plans, adjusting withdrawal strategies based on evolving needs, market conditions, and life expectancy.

6. **Professional Guidance**:
- Importance: Consulting financial advisors or retirement planning experts can provide personalized strategies.
- Strategy: Seek professional advice to tailor withdrawal plans to individual goals, risk tolerance, and financial situation.

By implementing thoughtful withdrawal strategies and considering various factors influencing longevity risk, individuals can enhance the likelihood of maintaining financial stability throughout their retirement, ensuring a comfortable and secure lifestyle even during extended life spans. Regular monitoring and adjustments are integral to the success of these strategies over the long term.

Adapting to Market Volatility

Adapting to market volatility is crucial for businesses to thrive in dynamic economic environments. Successful adaptation requires a comprehensive strategy that encompasses risk management, agility, and strategic planning.

Understanding Market Volatility

1. Market Analysis:
Conduct a thorough analysis of historical market trends and identify factors contributing to volatility. This includes economic indicators, geopolitical events, and industry-specific influences.

2. Risk Assessment:
Evaluate potential risks associated with market fluctuations. Categorize risks into short-term and long-term, and prioritize them based on their potential impact on your business.

Building Resilience

3. Diversification:
Create a diversified portfolio of products, services, or investments to spread risk. This can provide a buffer against downturns in specific markets and industries.

4. Financial Health:
Keep yourself in a strong financial position with enough cash on hand. This ensures your business can weather short-term shocks and capitalize on strategic opportunities during market downturns.

Implementing Adaptive Strategies

5. Agile Business Models:
Foster an agile organizational culture that allows for quick decision-making and flexibility in operations. This may involve streamlining processes and embracing technological advancements.

6. Scenario Planning:
Develop scenarios for different market conditions and create response plans for each scenario. This proactive approach enables the organization to react swiftly to changes.

Risk Management

7. Hedging Strategies:
Employ hedging strategies, such as financial instruments, to mitigate the impact of adverse market movements. This could involve currency hedging, commodity hedging, or interest rate hedging, depending on the nature of your business.

8. Insurance Coverage:
Evaluate and enhance insurance coverage to protect against unforeseen events. This may include business interruption insurance, liability coverage, or other policies tailored to specific risks.

Strategic Decision-Making

9. Data-Driven Decisions:
Leverage data analytics to make informed decisions. Monitor key performance indicators (KPIs) and use real-time data to adjust strategies in response to market changes.

10. Long-Term Vision:
Maintain a long-term strategic vision while adapting to short-term market fluctuations. This ensures that decisions align with overarching business goals.

Communication and Stakeholder Management

11. Transparency:
Maintain transparent communication with stakeholders, including employees, investors, and customers. Clearly articulate the organization's strategy for navigating market volatility.

12. Engaging Stakeholders:
Interact with important parties to get their opinions and insights. This collaborative approach can lead to innovative solutions and a better understanding of market dynamics.

In conclusion, adapting to market volatility requires a multifaceted approach that combines strategic planning, risk management, and a commitment to continuous improvement. By embracing change and proactively addressing challenges, businesses can position themselves to not only survive but thrive in volatile markets.

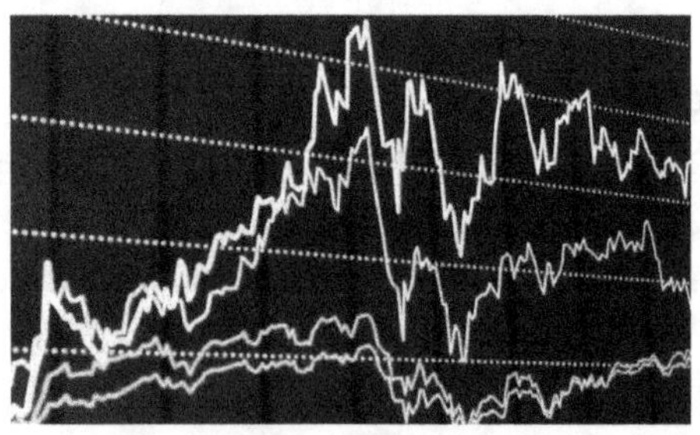

PART VII: Staying Active and Healthy

Maintaining an active and healthy lifestyle during retirement is essential for overall well-being and longevity. As individuals transition into this phase of life, it becomes paramount to focus on physical, mental, and social aspects of health. Here's a comprehensive guide:

Physical Well-Being

1. Regular Exercise:
Engage in a balanced exercise routine that includes cardiovascular activities (e.g., walking, swimming), strength training, and flexibility exercises. Consult with a fitness professional to create a personalized plan that aligns with your fitness level and health goals.

2. Outdoor Activities:
Take advantage of your free time to explore outdoor activities. This could involve hiking, cycling, gardening, or participating in group fitness classes. Outdoor activities not only promote physical health but also provide a refreshing change of environment.

Mental Health

3. Brain Stimulating Activities:
Take part in mentally stimulating activities to
maintain your mental acuity. Consider learning new
skills, participating in educational courses, or even
taking up hobbies that challenge your cognitive
abilities.

4. Mindfulness Practices:
 Include mindfulness exercises in your daily routine,
such as yoga or meditation. These activities can
reduce stress, improve focus, and contribute to
overall mental well-being.

Healthy Eating Habits

5. Balanced Nutrition:
Adopt a well-balanced diet rich in fruits, vegetables,
lean proteins, and whole grains. Consult with a
nutritionist to tailor your diet to meet your specific
nutritional needs, taking into account any health
conditions or dietary restrictions.

6. Meal Planning:
Plan your meals in advance to ensure a consistent
and nutritious diet. This not only supports physical
health but also contributes to maintaining a healthy
weight.

Social Engagement

7. Community Involvement:
Join local clubs, community organizations, or volunteer groups to stay socially active. The development and maintenance of social connections is important for mental and emotional health.

8. Family and Friendships:
Foster and strengthen relationships with family and friends. Spending quality time with loved ones provides emotional support and contributes to a sense of purpose and fulfillment.

Healthcare Maintenance

9. Regular Health Check-ups:
Schedule regular health check-ups to monitor and address any emerging health concerns. Early detection and intervention can significantly impact health outcomes.

10. Health Insurance:
Ensure that you have comprehensive health insurance coverage. This provides financial security in case of unexpected medical expenses and encourages regular health check-ups.

Leisure and Enjoyment

11. Travel and Exploration:
Take advantage of your retirement to travel and explore new places. Traveling not only provides leisure but also broadens your horizons and introduces you to new cultures and experiences.

12. Recreational Pursuits:
Pursue recreational activities that bring you joy, whether it's playing a musical instrument, painting, or participating in a book club. These activities contribute to a fulfilling and enjoyable retirement.

In conclusion, a holistic approach to staying active and healthy during retirement involves a combination of physical activity, mental stimulation, social engagement, healthy eating, and proactive healthcare. By incorporating these elements into your lifestyle, you can enhance the quality of your retirement years and ensure a fulfilling and vibrant post-work life.

Healthcare Navigation in Retirement

As individuals transition into retirement, navigating the healthcare landscape becomes a crucial aspect of ensuring a healthy and secure future. This guide aims to provide a detailed overview of healthcare considerations, options, and strategies for retirees, offering a roadmap for making informed decisions.

Understanding Medicare:
One cornerstone of healthcare in retirement is Medicare, the federal health insurance program for individuals aged 65 and older. Familiarize yourself with the different parts of Medicare: Part A (hospital insurance), Part B (medical insurance), Part C (Medicare Advantage), and Part D (prescription drug coverage). Understanding these components is essential for making informed enrollment decisions.

Medigap and Supplemental Insurance:
While Medicare covers many healthcare costs, it doesn't cover everything. Medigap plans (Medicare Supplement Insurance) can help fill the gaps by covering expenses like deductibles and copayments. Research and compare different Medigap plans to choose the one that best aligns with your healthcare needs and financial situation.

Long-Term Care Planning:
Planning for potential long-term care needs is vital in retirement. Long-term care insurance can help cover the costs of services like nursing home care, assisted living, and home healthcare. Evaluate your options and consider your preferences to make well-informed decisions about long-term care coverage.

Medicaid Considerations:
For retirees with limited financial resources, Medicaid can be a critical source of healthcare coverage. Understanding Medicaid eligibility criteria and planning accordingly can provide a safety net for individuals facing financial challenges in retirement.

Health Savings Accounts (HSAs) and Retirement:
Maximizing the benefits of Health Savings Accounts (HSAs) during your working years can contribute to a healthcare fund for retirement. HSAs offer tax advantages, and funds can be used for qualified medical expenses in retirement. Explore the potential benefits of contributing to an HSA throughout your career.

Wellness and Preventive Care:
Prioritizing wellness and preventive care is essential for maintaining good health in retirement. Consider incorporating healthy habits into your lifestyle, staying up-to-date on vaccinations, and

scheduling regular check-ups. Wellness-focused initiatives can contribute to a higher quality of life during retirement.

Telehealth and Technological Solutions:
Explore technological advancements in healthcare, such as telehealth services, which can enhance accessibility to medical professionals. Familiarize yourself with digital health tools and platforms that can facilitate remote monitoring and communication with healthcare providers.

Legal and End-of-Life Healthcare Planning:
Ensure your healthcare wishes are documented through legal tools like advance directives and living wills. Discuss your preferences with family members and ensure they are aware of your medical wishes. Planning for end-of-life care can provide peace of mind and ensure that your healthcare decisions align with your values.

Conclusion
Healthcare navigation in retirement requires a multifaceted approach, encompassing Medicare enrollment, supplemental insurance considerations, long-term care planning, and a commitment to preventive care. By proactively addressing healthcare needs and staying informed about available options, retirees can cultivate a secure and healthy lifestyle in their later years.

PART VIII: Conclusion

Embracing Retirement with Confidence

Embracing retirement with confidence is a significant life transition that requires careful planning and a positive mindset. Here are key aspects to consider:

Financial Preparedness:

1. Budgeting and Planning:

   - Develop a comprehensive budget that outlines your anticipated expenses and income during retirement.

   - Consider consulting with a financial advisor to ensure your investments align with your retirement goals.

2. Emergency Fund:

   - Maintain an emergency fund to cover unexpected expenses and to provide a financial safety net during retirement.

3. Healthcare Planning:

   - Assess healthcare needs and explore insurance options to ensure comprehensive coverage during retirement.

Lifestyle Adjustment:

1. Hobbies and Interests:

   - Identify and cultivate hobbies and interests that can provide fulfillment and purpose in retirement.

2. Social Connections:

- Foster and maintain social connections to combat isolation. Consider joining clubs or community groups to stay engaged.

3. Travel Plans:

- Plan for travel experiences that align with your interests. This can be an excellent way to explore new places and create lasting memories.

Emotional and Mental Well-being:

1. Mindfulness and Relaxation:

- Embrace mindfulness practices, such as meditation or yoga, to promote emotional well-being and stress management.

2. Goal Setting:

- Set realistic and achievable goals for yourself during retirement. This could be learning a new skill, volunteering, or pursuing a passion project.

3. Professional Guidance:

- Seek guidance from retirement counselors or therapists to navigate the emotional aspects of this life transition.

Legal and Estate Planning:

1. Will and Estate:

- Review and update your will and estate plans to ensure your wishes are documented and legally sound.

2. Power of Attorney:
   - Designate powers of attorney for healthcare and financial matters to trusted individuals.

Continued Learning:
1. Education and Training:
   - Consider opportunities for continued learning, such as workshops or classes, to keep your mind active and engaged.

2. Adaptability:
   - Embrace adaptability as a key skill. Be open to new experiences and challenges, as they contribute to personal growth.

Regular Assessments:
1. Financial Checkups:
   - Conduct regular financial checkups to ensure your retirement plan remains aligned with your evolving needs and goals.

2. Life Goals:
   - Periodically reassess your life goals and adjust your retirement plans accordingly. Adapting to changing conditions requires flexibility.

By addressing these aspects comprehensively, you can approach retirement with confidence, knowing that you have a well-rounded plan that encompasses financial stability, emotional well-being, and a purposeful lifestyle.

www.ingramcontent.com/pod-product-compliance
Lightning Source LLC
Chambersburg PA
CBHW082345270726
48658CB00017B/3129